# IT'S OKAY TO FAIL

*Bold Decisions of a Young Life ...*

Drishti Bajaj

INDIA • SINGAPORE • MALAYSIA

# Dedication

To the failures that made me hit rock bottom,
To the endless loop of questioning my choices,
To doubting my capabilities and falling apart,
This book is an ode to my mini-share of struggles.

# CONTENTS

# Acknowledgements

This very book is my first baby that took more than 9 months to come to life. The feeling is priceless to say the least.

Thanking my life experiences and people I met on the journey would be like a series of understatements.

However, let's try, because you know what, even though it's okay to fail you can never fail at expressing your gratitude to those you love :)

My A1 since day 1 has to be my sister. I will not say she's my second mother but a ball of energy that forces me to think positive in all pathetic situations.

We have lived in the same room for years and behaved like arrogant roommates, and we have also bonded so well like there's no third person on the planet.

She has been available for me despite time zone differences, flight layovers and her medicine exams. Oh, btw, she's a physiotherapist who fixes the nerves of my brain over a video call from Boston.

My Mom and Dad are an absolute definition of Indian household parents with a major addition of the fact that they are blindly supportive towards both me and my sister.

When I compare what my parents do with the usual Indian households, I mean they cannot knock on the door of my room, they cannot stop calling my nickname at places they should avoid and of course they cannot let me stay far away from them. I know, I can see you heading your head too, because all our parents are cut from the same cloth I guess!

I would also want to add my special special gratitude to the pillars of discipline and perfection that my both grand-dads were, my dada and nana. The ship would be at stake without these two. And the fuel to these ships are dadi and nani. These women are absolute gems and way ahead of their times.

These people have contributed their sweat, blood and skills to make me who I am today.

This book is a gift for my children and the children of my family—both sides to know their mom, aunt, bua, masi, mami and 10,000 other relations was so cool back in the day. And still is. Forever will be. Never waning, never weeding out, and never being afraid of failure :)

This book has a lot to offer if you make the right use of lessons mentioned.

These lessons are curated by observing life from my lens and my chosen bunch of friends have added immense value to shape my choices in different walks of life.

Thank you to my friends since childhood and teenage, your loyalty, love and laughter have shaped my world in ways I can never fully express.

The list stands in no particular order but names pop-up in my head as I write this today.

Megha, Akshay, Punit, Shefali, Deven, Kirti, Shraddha, Rajiv, Nishit, Sagar, Ravi, Juhi, Ayush, Harshita, Karuna, Tamanna, Atith, Maitry, Titiksha, Gurkirat, Anisha, Rahul, Nihar, Yash, Jay, Richard, Arvind, Siddhesh, Aashi, Devyani, Rohit, Richi, Azvi, Soham, Dnyanesh, Parth

In the end, I want to thank the gems I've found in the form of my teachers and mentors - kindergarten to school to junior college to post graduation.

And I have utmost respect for a mentor I have found late in life- Mohit Geat, who is also my Jeetu Bhaiya, literally.

# Who is this book for?

This book is for anyone who has had a big goal in life and has failed at it.

This book is for anyone who is looking for inspiration but can't find it anywhere. This book is for every single person who still believes in themselves even if no one else does.

Through the pages of this book, we will speak about my journey in CA. I faced multiple failures in the process.

As I sat down to reflect on them for the purpose of this book, I figured they aren't just my failures.

Every single one of us goes through failures.

As the cliche (but true) statement goes: Failures really are the stepping stones to success!

So, even if you are not pursuing CA, what I can say for sure is that you have faced or are going to face failures on your way in life.

Please don't get me wrong. I only have blessings and good wishes for you. I am simply stating some facts, that some failures are fodder for success. One person's failure is another person's fuel.

I want this book and half-a-decade of my failures to be the guiding light for you, so you may realise:

*It's okay to fail.*

*Absolutely. Unflinchingly. Unabashedly. OKAY to fail.*

There is so much more on the other side. Most of which you don't even realise, unless you are okay to fail.

**In this book, we will speak about how it is okay to fail. You are much bigger than what the world defines as success.**

And have the power to create your own version of success. Like I have. So can you :)

On that note, let's go :))

# Preface: Hi, it's D

Hi, I am Drishti.

Here's a little disclaimer: The views in this book are personal and the experiences shared are real.

I work at the intersection of Content and Strategy. And I work next to a founder in a startup. And I am also preparing for my MBA.

Experience and all is good, but you need a fancy degree, right? If not CA, why not MBA? The grind shouldn't stop friends!

I am super grateful for the fact that I get to work from home most days of the week, while preparing for my MBA. All of this, after dealing with bruises and burns of quitting CA should anyway deserve an award :)

But that is my present.

We are hardly defined by our present.

What truly defines us in the present is our past.

And my past, like the past of most of us, was painful.

Okay not childhood trauma or struggling to pay for my education (thank you, Mom and Dad). However, a lot of self-inflicted trauma (thank you, myself)

I am also not talking about a romantic heartbreak. Some of us are lucky to move on from that heartbreak and find a sweetheart we truly love.

I am rather talking about my academic heartbreak—of not being able to clear CA. After giving it multiple days, nights, weeks, months, years, local train journeys, metro train journeys, and journeys of checking the CA results website for half a decade, in the hope of a positive result, I am still not on the other side of making these two letters my prefix.

There is no "moving on" from here.

Or maybe there is. By writing a book on it!

People who are not able to clear CAT (the entrance exam for IIMs) usually try for GMAT. If they make it, they can still make it to the premium colleges in the world.

Fortunately and unfortunately, there is no doorway like this when you pursue CA.

It's a failure for those who so wanted to clear CA, but freedom for people like me who did not listen to their intuition for the longest time. And missed out on so much fun (and money) pursuing something else!

But this book is not about complaining about why I couldn't clear CA.

Rather, this book is about how I created a totally different world when I didn't fit into the world of CA, instead of knocking at its door incessantly and losing my hope and energy in the process.

Well, I did lose hope and knocked at the door of CA incessantly for half a decade, but, when the penny did drop, I was able to catch a lot more.

This book is about how you must listen to your heart and (sometimes) perhaps not listen to your loved ones and do what you know is your true calling. Of course, please maintain the sanity of making sure you are not financially dependent on your parents.

This book is about knowing that just because I failed at CA, does not mean I am incapable or it makes CAs better than me or my alternative career better than CA. It simply means I am a rockstar of the work I do, like we all should be.

I am not a celebrity. Or an influencer. Or Orry.

I am just like you. A girl next door. With big hopes, ambitions and dreams. With failures under her belt. (And in the book you are holding in your hand.) And with (slightly powerful) courage to give up when I knew it was not right to persist, and the indomitable will to fight hard when persistence is the most important thing I need.

I am just like you.

Or maybe I am not. Remember—same same, but different?

Through this book, I do not intend to give you any pathbreaking knowledge to change your life. Man, I am only 24!

But if my story gives you a hope to go fight your failures, whether it is figuring a new way out or being bold to share her failures in public, I think I would have done my job well.

In a world where everyone works hard for 50 years to write a book on their success story, I think I should finally give myself a pat on the back to write a book on my failures, at less than half that age!

PS: That pat on the back is especially needed, especially after the pain in my back with the weights of CA books!

With that, let's begin an unscripted, unseen, unfiltered story of my FaceTime with failure, zero regrets, and having the courage to forge my own path, when the path forged for me did not work out.

# Chapter 1

# Before We Start, a Sneak Peek Into the World of CA

Since we are going to be talking about my journey into the world of CA, I'll take a bit to make you understand how the course operates.

It's simple. Anyone can understand it. The course has three stages:

Stage 1: CPT or The Common Proficiency Test. It is the entrance exam of Multiple Choice Questions.

You can appear for it immediately after clearing your $12^{th}$ grade exams.

Stage 2: CA Inter

It is the second stage of CA, which you may appear for after 9 months of clearing the CPT exam.

It is extremely tough. Usually what the world calls "CA is tough", they mean it starts here. While people fail in the CPT stage as well, it is in Inter that the failure rate goes high drastically. When you do fail, you are eligible to reappear after 6 months (now 4 months).

Every time you appear for the exam, it is called an "attempt". In CA, "attempt" is called the nth time when you are appearing for the same exam. So if you cleared

CA Inter after appearing in it for the third time, you are said to have cleared Inter in 3rd attempt.

I appeared for Inter in May 2018, November 2018, May 2019, November 2019, January 2021 (changed schedule due to the Covid pandemic), May 2022 and November 2022.

And failed.

Through the pages of this book, you will learn about my journey and juggling with failures and self-doubts through these attempts, until I finally decided to give up.

The Inter stage has 8 subjects, divided into Group 1 and Group 2, with 4 subjects each.

Why am I telling this to you? Because if 8 subjects seem to be too much of a cognitive load, you are free to appear for either group in one attempt, and then appear for the other group in the second attempt.

Once you clear the Inter stage, you are eligible for 2 things:

- To start the 3-year long articleship (which has now become 2) with a practising CA. It is to get on-the-ground learnings into the practical problems CA solve

- You now enter the toughest stage of life and CA—CA Final

Stage 3: CA Final: As the name suggests, once you clear this stage, which also has 8 subjects, 4 in each group, you become a Chartered Accountant.

I could not get myself to enter the Final stage or get into articleship, so most of what you will learn from me through the pages of this book is all about CA Inter.

All of these have some more depth to it, but I guess we are fine with understanding these basics of CA, and dive right into the book.

It is also noteworthy to mention that some stages of CA get modified in a few years like they have right now, which you may easily check out on the website of The Institute of Chartered Accountants of India (ICAI).

However, since what I explained above was what was applicable to me (and is what we talk about in the book), I hope the book will now do a good job of making you understand my state of mind.

Nothing in the book is technical.

***Everything is an internal journey.***

Which is why, I am super excited to share this with you. On that note, let's begin!!

# Chapter 2

# Why CA as a Career?

Why did I choose CA as a career? What inspired me to get there?

Of all the things that the world has to offer, why the choice of one of the toughest courses to clear?

Okay, let's get to the point without going round and round in circles.

If you become a CA, the path is laid with money, fame and recognition.

If you fail to become a CA, you can write a book and then again get to a place of having money, fame and recognition.

No matter what the result is, there isglory and gorgeousness on either side :)

But jokes apart, now as I think about it, there were two things that led to me deciding if I wanted to pick up CA as a career:

1.  During the days of annual return filing, I used to see my father stay on long phone calls with his CA. There were times when he was very frustrated because the CA could not complete the return

filing for my father on time, which even led to my father paying penalties sometimes. Looking at all of this, I told myself, "If I, through my career, could not take the frustration away from my Dad, was it even worth it?"

Now as I look at it, I tell myself: Bro, you could find another CA for him! Easy peezy lemon squeezy.

***Lesson learnt later:*** Please put oxygen masks on your face first before helping others. Please pursue a career of your choice and help yourself out before you help out your family and friends with your career.

2.   Of course, there is money in the profession.

Look, you can be an (Anil) Ambani and still be bankrupt. But having studied (and cleared) Statistics in CPT stage and gone through the law of averages, most CAs make enviable money. Yes, including the ones you think don't make any money. Unlike the world has made us believe the lies, I do not think pursuing money is a bad thing.

***There's nothing nobler than giving yourself a good life and inspiring others to do the same.***

***Lesson learnt later:*** The opportunity cost of not listening to my intuition and wanting to take away my father's frustration led me to not making any money during those few years.

Also, the probability of making money doing what you love and enjoy is higher than doing something just for the sake of external validation.

If we flash back a little, in the 9th standard I had a choice to pick up an optional subject. I went ahead with my heart and picked up Fine Arts. Today I am glad I did that. However, for the longest time during my CA preparation days I used to think I should have picked up Commercial Applications, as it had basics of Accounting and Finance.

Today, after wandering through the multitude of failures, I am so glad I was not

"adult" enough to give logic a chance.

That is what failure does to you. It makes you regret all your past choices even if they worked out, and makes you think things would have been different had you done different things.

But another thing failure does to you is make you realise that listening to your heart and not going on with logic is the most logical way to success in life.

Something I realised quite late.

# Chapter 3

# Hormonal Changes, House Changes, Heart Changes

I was born and brought up in Kalyan, Maharashtra.

My elder sister and I, with our parents and grandparents around, life was pretty good.

I went to a day-boarding school. The Meridian School in Kalyan, where I would study for 7 years of my formative years. We would have swimming and all sorts of extracurricular activities at the school. We would also have our breakfast, lunch and even snacks over there. We were legit living with our friends. In 2nd standard, my first overnight trip away from family was also from that school.

I also started learning Bharatanatyam, the dance form in the same school. (The art was oozing out of me, way before I forced myself to become a CA for so many years!) I even went on to win an award for my performance on "Breathless" by Shankar Mahadevan.

Till date, when I think of "school" that school comes to my mind.

When I was 13 years old, our entire family — consisting of my parents, my grandparents, my elder sister, and me — moved to Thane.

The idea was to be a part of Mumbai. (Thane happens to be a suburb, an extension of Mumbai).

To aid my sister's higher education.

And of course, to have a platform for my higher education as well. It was a time I was going through multiple changes in my life.

When you are 13, you are going through puberty. Not only your hormones, you are

also learning to walk with a pad or a cup between your thighs for 16% of the month and walk normally! What?! Is that all adult women do for almost 4 decades of their lives? If being a female did not come with its own sense of fighting for positions in the workplace, you also have to maintain the correct positions almost every month. Dear God, why?

Also, as a teenager you are anyway beginning to realise how almost everything is screwed up.

Then came this shifting of home.

Teenage had uprooted me from my childhood already. Now I was also uprooted from my childhood home.

As well as my school, which was my real home.

Even though it was good for us, I really wonder how many of the good things we run after are really good.

Mumbai was too fast.

The crowd in my new school always seemed to be in a hurry to "achieve".

I was trying to fit in.

Perhaps I wasn't aware of this back then, but too many life-altering events at the same time are not as beautiful as they appear to be.

You lose so many things that are a part of you. So much so, that you do not recognise yourself, except your face, which has also lost its joy. Maybe you are a Joey in Chandler Bing's body :)

Anyway, a year later, when I was almost trying to settle in, came another choice of picking subjects for Class 9.

The available choices were Fine Arts, Computer Applications, Economic Applications and Commercial Applications.

I loved Fine Arts, so I went ahead with it. Even talking about it today brings a smile on my face :))

I also went on to score 86 marks in 10th Boards in Fine Arts — a score I was proud of.

But I think I was naive enough to not know that I should pursue a career in Fine Arts instead of CA. Bro, the marks and the Bharatnatyam award were not enough to convince me? Did I want Leonardo da Vinci to rise from his grave to tell me to pursue arts? Or maybe I wanted to get into a train and expect Geet from Jab

We Met to convince me. She was great at convincing, wasn't she? :)

However, by now, the logical mind had taken over.

Which is where my decision making of picking CA as a course began :)

"It's the start, of something new;

It feels so right, to be here with you"

This is the very first song in the very first High School Musical movie of the High School Musical trilogy.

Trust me, my next journey felt exactly the opposite of it. Because it wasn't right. And it took a lot of wrong decisions to know that right…

# Chapter 4

# How I Picked Up CA as a Career

When you are an aspirational kid in a normal household in India where (in the time I grew up) the father makes money and takes care of the family's financial needs.

While mom is a homemaker and takes care of the family's emotional needs.

As a kid, you want to do everything in your life to make sure you reduce both your parents' burden.

A burden they never carried as a burden, but something responsible kids want to reduce for them anyway.

Which is exactly what I wanted to be for my father, in my career.

Every year, at the time of return filing, all of a sudden the importance of CA in my father's life would increase.

Not only that, I have seen my father sitting frustrated on a call with his CA, almost exhausted.

In another instance, I used to hate it when my father used to refer to someone as "seth" / "sahab" over the phone. It used to irk me because why would he treat someone superior to him, I would wonder. (He still does so, not out of inferiority but out of respect. Just that I have understood it now :))

Looking at him and not being able to help him out, I decided I will become a CA.

It was more of an emotional decision than a well thought-out decision, because hey, you want to fight the world to make sure you don't see your parents frustrated with or because of anyone else.

Also, just like parents realise it later on, even though they could do the best of things for their kids and provide them with everything, each kid goes on to make their destiny through their choices and karma.

Similarly, years after making this decision (when I finally quit) I realised that the only way to make sure that my father was not frustrated, was to pick a career I wasn't frustrated with.

Seeing me struggle day after day, attempt after attempt, year after year was perhaps making him more frustrated.

Also, my father happens to be a construction contractor, where he takes care of government projects and private buildings.

Though he never said it explicitly, I had heard things from his colleagues, stating "in

2-1 years I would be capable of joining him in office and be his right hand."

Now as I look back, I realise we should not take everything that our parents say, seriously. We anyway don't take it seriously when they ask us to switch off the TV, go to a satsang with them or attend a family function. But with our careers, we take their silence (in their life) seriously! Seriously, each one of us who does that should get an award for hypocrisy. Starting with myself :)

It might sound counterintuitive, but it takes courage to accept that our parents are also human beings, just like us.

Their words might sometimes be unpremeditated, just like ours.

So it's okay if we are not able to make all their words come true. Plus, they might even have spoken those words when they might be tired, had a long day, or were frustrated with someone else. Maybe they didn't mean it in the first place! Just like sometimes we don't mean what we say. It is just an impulse response.

On the same accord, our parents also didn't say that they were flexible with everything, as long as it kept you happy. But they mean it, right?

*The absence and presence of words means a lot more than what we see on the surface.*

*Sometimes some realisations take years (and attempts) to come. And any realisation and awareness is better late than never.*

# Chapter 5

# Communication Solves for Most Problems

As I look back on why I wanted to be a CA despite early (and loud) signs of why it was not meant for me in the first place, I think a part of me wanted to make my parents proud.

Little did I know, I would be able to make them proud when I would be happy in the first place!

You see, I am blessed to have parents who are pretty chill. I know a lot of other people don't have that privilege, but I should have used mine, when I wanted to.

We shifted our homes from Kalyan to Thane, just to have proximity to my sister's college, which was KJ Somaiya. By the way, in Kalyan, our home was on the 4th floor of the same building whose ground floor was my father's office.

That would not have been an easy move for him at all. But he did.

Once our family was due to go for a vacation to Bali just before my CPT exams, which they didn't cancel because after that my sister's college would have started. Of course, I missed the vacation out of choice.

The point I am trying to make is that my family is indeed "pretty cool" but I couldn't gather the courage to tell them, a very simple sentence.

"This ain't working. We gotta switch." I should have.

I don't know why.

Or maybe I do.

Here's a secret:

When the result of my CPT exam was out, I was in my college. The moment I called up my father to tell him that I had cleared, he came over to my college (not immediately, we live in Mumbai lol, but he left his place immediately to come to my college.)

I still remember the feeling when he came over to my college to congratulate me, and then we both went home together to have a family celebration.

It was a day I'd never forget.

Bro, whose father comes to their college to pick them up? Mine!

Or how often do you have these family celebrations together?

Or you felt so happy in the moment that you let the numbers overtake your heart –which for me lied in arts more than commerce.

All through the Inter attempts when I kept telling myself "once more" or "this time I will crack it" or "let's just give ourselves one more chance", a part of me was waiting for my father to come to me to celebrate again.

I had forgotten, he was already there for me, and I kept waiting for him still.

# Chapter 6

# Sometimes, You Ought to Unfollow the Crowd

I pursued my graduation from HR College in Mumbai, which is the hub for producing Chartered Accountants.

When you are in an environment like that, you almost attract raised brows when you are doing something different.

After all, together means safe. Together means no need to reinvent the wheel. Together means you don't need to think, you just go where everywhere else goes. Huh, together we should perhaps scrap this trap of "together".

Because you don't give your exams together.

In your exam hall, you are alone.

In your CA preparation days, you are alone.

In your early mornings and late nights and incessant local train rides and changing syllabus and crippling self-doubt and unable to see a future path after multiple failed attempts — you are alone. All alone.

You know how that feels? Overwhelming. Insignificant. Withdrawn.

Which is why we all should embrace our uniqueness from the start. Since you are going to be alone, at least take your passion and uniqueness with you, which will wake up, sleep, eat with you, quietly cleanse your tears when you have self-doubts, and will remind you consistently that you are bigger than the tiny rock you can't see beyond at the moment.

If you go where the crowd is, you will end up at the same place where everywhere is and is probably pretending to be happy, when they are also wondering if they landed at the right place!

This almost looks like I am criticising one of the most premium institutes of the country. Nothing could be further from the truth.

I was rather smitten by HR college.

When I applied to HR college (junior college) after clearing my 10th board exams, I was very little away from the cutoff percentage. The cutoff was ~80% while I had obtained 77.87%.

So what I did was I shared a national level dance certificate where I had secured second position as a solo dancer (Remember—Bharatnatyam on Breathless?) with the Admin of the HR college over email.

The application was exactly like a B-school application where I tried to sell them why I am the right fit for them.

I think this is what got me in. Part persistence. Part love for art. Part of me knocking on the door again and again so the other person had to let me in.

Oh, I wish I had that relentlessness when I needed it the most. I would have quit sooner. *But sometimes the most important parts of you get buried when you need them the most.*

So they can eventually bloom for the rest of your life…

# Chapter 7

# Sometimes, Borderline Failure is a Huge Sign

I secured 106 marks out of 200 in CPT. The passing marks used to be 100.

In the subject of Mathematics, also called Quantitative Aptitude. I secured 16 marks out of 50, where the passing marks were 15.

I was crazy happy when I cleared CPT.

I worked very hard.

Studied as if I would not study again.

Missed on a family vacation to Bali, while my family went ahead.

You see, clearing CPT gave me everything in return for what I had sacrificed for.

However, I have learnt that human beings make their biggest mistakes in periods of extreme happiness and extreme sadness.

Which is what I did.

When I cleared CPT, I did not sit down to make me understand:

- I had no idea of what real CA is, CPT was merely an aptitude test. If I was working this hard for the last 3 months, I had no idea what the next 12 months would bring.

- 106 marks is still borderline failure, despite working so hard and sacrificing all that I hadn't thought. I would not say that people who have secured ~100 marks or so in CPT would not become CA. I am sure there must be many. However, my life was mine to reflect, no one else's.

- I went with the flow of students in HR college. HR college is also called a CA factory, so what do I do if I do not do what everyone is doing? I wasn't Apple that I could think different. Only to realise later, thinking different is what will make us unique like Apple.

As I look back, I think we should develop the ability to pause and reflect after every success and failure, and ask ourselves:

What do I want? What do I really really want?

You will anyway be working hard and making a lot of sacrifices, so why not do it towards what you want, and not follow the crowd?

The answer, I tell you, is not easy.

However, life becomes easy when you do what you want to do.

It's a skill that only becomes more useful with practice.

For me, practice meant several attempts (and years) slogging at Inter ● ‹›`'

Reminds me of how everyone on social media who promises you to be rich, is rich. Rarely do we see examples of people becoming rich by following those who promise you to be rich.

In career (and in life) every level demands a different level of commitment and dedication from you.

***Your past is an inspiration, not a point of validation for future success.***

And your past is also a mirror, which your future might become if you don't change what is in the present.

Isn't it a beautiful present?

# Chapter 8

# If Failure Leaves Clues, Success Also Leaves Clues

In India, cricket is the oxygen of sports.

Sometimes, to the point of people trolling the top stars like Virat Kohli to worship them when they win an important match.

However, what remains constant is the best cricketers go on to perform despite the trolls being thrown to them by the entire nation.

Why am I telling this to you in a book about my CA journey? I have a reason…

When I was pursuing my CPT, I was hardly focused on the results. I did not even think about them.

What I did was focus on the process.

*Consistency.*

*Working hard.*

*Having discipline, and following it.*

*Showing up to do the process of the routine.*

*Put blinders on everything, and be focused as a frontline soldier.*

That is why, despite so many signs that I should not have done CA, I ended up clearing CPT.

There is a magic, a miracle that takes you to a result when you care the least about it. Yet, you put in the effortless effort because that is the only thing you can control.

If there were early signs that I should not have gone ahead with CA, as I shared in the previous chapter, there were also early signs how I should have approached my studies once I did pick it up.

While I was pursuing Inter, I was everything I was not while pursuing CPT.

I was focused on the results.

I was trying very very hard to get them.

I did not follow a routine like I did while pursuing CPT.

My body also used to give up through cycles of extreme productivity and lack of it. I lost a sense of being at one with myself.

It is an important thing to work very hard, it is another thing to forget yourself in the process.

I did the latter, which was unlike my "success mantra" that I developed in CPT.

This is something you could learn from cricketers. They didn't get into cricket in order to reap the fame, fortune and fantasy that being a famous cricketer in India comes with.

They were in it for the process. They were in it for the joy of cricket.

They were in it because they did not know who they would be, if they were not a cricketer.

This is something that now goes on to become a life lesson for me. Work hard. Very hard. But enjoy the process equally.

If you aren't enjoying it, either the process needs to change or the goal.

Like I have learnt an important lesson: Your life is always speaking to you.

# Chapter 9

# Early Signs: Isn't Life Always Speaking to You?

Here's a confession: I never really wanted to become a CA.

As a matter of fact, when there were only 5 days left for enrolment for CPT, I enrolled on the 4th day. Almost on the edge.

All I wanted to do was go to the ISME.

When I was in junior college in my 11th standard at HR college, we were taken to a field visit at ISME college.

It turns out, Dr. Indu Shahani, who was the Principal of HR College from 2000-2016, was also the founding dean of the Indian School of Management & Entrepreneurship (ISME).

And man do I tell you, I was smitten by her! Still am. Perhaps forever will be.

On our visit to ISME, she conducted a masterclass on entrepreneurship. It wasn't just a session, it was a much-needed confidence and perspective that people my age need. She got the best-in-class faculty to India, tied up with B-schools abroad to solve for global exposure here in India, and was never scared of inventing new ways of teaching.

Located in Lower Parel back then (now in Bandra Kurla Complex), the ISME was surrounded by corporate offices in its surroundings. So even if you did not try, you would certainly run into a CXO and have a conversation with them.

If there is one hill I am willing to die on, it is this: The people you surround yourself with are going to determine everything about you:

*Your mindset.*

*The money you make. Your emotional state*

*Even your physical health.*

Which is why, my heart and my lungs were shouting out ISME loudly.

However, back then ISME did not offer a degree course, only a diploma course. (Update: As on date they have gotten accredited and recognised by the University Grants Commission, become a degree course and also changed the nomenclature to Atlas Skilltech University.)

However, my father, like any father, would rightly expect his daughter to go for a degree. Even though it was a conventional mindset, I think it was not worth the risk for him. After all, back in his days we didn't pick our colleges to bump into CXOs and to like our Principals, did we?

I could not get a buy-in from him.

Since we did not get a heads up for ISME, CA, here we come!

In life, I have figured, if you want to do something meaningful, you have to be the person who shows up every day.

You have to love the hard work.

You have to put your 150% into what you do. And at a moment you are exhausted, you have to put in even more.

Which is why it is important to do what you enjoy doing.

Because if you are going to work hard anyway, why not work hard on something that makes you come alive?

A lot of us postpone doing the things we want to do, thinking "when I will have this, I will do this…"

Maybe some of us have real problems that we have to go through the grind.

However, for the rest of us, we are perhaps creating our problems by becoming our problems.

The only thing we often need in moments of doubts, is getting out of our own way. And focus on joy.

As of writing this book, I had moved out of my safe space, my home and the city of dreams Mumbai, to work in Pune, because I work directly with the CEO of a company.

Even though the work was hybrid and I oscillated between Mumbai and Pune for almost a year, I enjoyed it.

Will I be doing it 5 years hence? I don't know.

Will I be focusing on joy 5 years hence?

Learning from my multiple failures (which you will read in the coming chapters): Hell yes.

# Chapter 10

# The Bermuda Triangle of Bad Decisions

When you are preparing for a course as difficult as CA, making decisions based on

"lucky charm" without having a strategy in place is disastrous.

Which is exactly what I did, when I picked up coaching for Inter 48,756 miles away from my home!!

Thane. Andheri. 22 Kms. However, how did we land there? Let us go there step-by-step.

This is the time when I have enrolled for the CA course. The next steps were:

1. Figure out where to go for coaching.

2. Pay extra attention to Mathematics. Fun-fact: I had already picked Mathematics in 11th grade, but it wasn't my cup of tea. Thus, I dropped it in 12th standard, because it would then affect my grades. Yes, I made a wise choice for my grades in 12th standard, but for my career, CA, I spent 5 years for it! Life is humorous in its own ways, people!!

3.  Learn to balance this new life! (Gasps.) I went
    ahead with the obvious choice:

My Uncle (my Mom's sister's (Masi as we call in Hindi)
husband) was teaching at a coaching class in Andheri
for more than a decade.

Because he was family, it almost felt like the obvious
choice to go study from him. Because I needed help
with Mathematics, I could also take extra tuitions over
there. Seemed like a perfect fit.

There was just one problem though:

We used to live in Thane. The coaching was in
Andheri.

The duration was 1.5 hours on one side, covering
distance by local train, metro and walking on foot!

However, I managed to cover that distance during
CPT.

The coaching was only for two months. Also very
rewarding. We used to solve our scanners in class,
together. Our teachers would provide us revision
sessions. We would have tiny tests. Even though we
were all quite competitive, we were like a family. For the
two-and-a-half months we were taking the coachings,
we were literally together from mornings to evenings.
We helped each other. There was no room for jealousy
or mockery. Pure friendships. Friendships where each
wanted to grow without kicking the other.

It was a mess I had no stress in. Also, I was fresh to this whirlwind.

When you are new in the pool, even going upstream seems like "you're supposed to do it."

While I cleared CPT eventually, the journey to Inter was not going to be an easy one. Now is the time to explore it bit by bit, bird by bird :)

# Chapter 11

# Inter, Here We Come!

If you don't know by now, I felt like I had conquered the world when I cleared CPT. Little did I know, it wasn't even a city.

When I entered Inter, it was a different planet altogether. Look, we all have cleared levels in school.

Go from one standard to another.

One class to the next.

You have teachers to teach you everything. You learn.

You give the exams.

You go on to the next level. Pretty straightforward, huh? Except, it is not.

***In CA, the level of commitment, studies and discipline that are expected of you don't grow in a linear manner, they grow exponentially.***

Plus, I had so much going through for myself.

My first attempt of Inter was May 2018, and here are are some of the things I was going through:

- GST was now introduced in our syllabus. Everything felt new. As if it wasn't already!

- Travelling from Thane to Churchgate for college, and then from Churchgate to Andheri for coaching every day was overwhelming. Or maybe overwhelming is an underwhelming word! Okay I should have looked for a coaching nearby, but you rarely recognise the life lessons while you are in the middle of them :)

- The classes would get over at 7.30 pm, but since that was the rush hour in Mumbai local, I would often stay back along with one of my friends (Harshita Oza, who is now a CA) until 9.30 pm, and then drag my exhausted mind and body to the heroic commute again.

- Switching from secretarial practice and no Maths background, with Costing being a 100-mark paper was another feather to the cap of surprises.

- I was late to home for dinner, and missed all of daily family dinners, something the 6 of us (my sister and I, our parents and grandparents) would initially have together, no matter what. I thus started having dosa for dinner next to Versova station. My friend Tamanna, who is now a CA, would be my partner in crime. She now has the CA degree. And I have a book :) (Well, considering so few CAs actually write their book, I have fallen in love with this weird achievement of mine!)

- The study modules arrived in November 2017 for the May 2018 attempt, which was remarkably late.

- I was all of 17 years old!

Clearly, there was a lot that was not working out for me.

I would not be mean to say it was all the fault of situations and people, and I was just showing up, but things were not being aligned.

Of course, I could make better decisions.

Or speak about it to my family. Or speak to my uncle. Or any other mentor at coaching classes. Or anyone else online. Dude, it was 2017, not 1917!

You don't need to have all the answers with you. I get it.

But you need to learn how to figure out answers. Especially if the problems at hand require more than what you are able to solve.

Which I believe, is something I could fix if I could go back to the moment.

Or maybe not, and let everyone (myself included) draw a leaf from this for our future decisions.

After all, a life lesson learnt is a mistake minted to its best.

# Chapter 12

# Sometimes the Problem is Not the Problem

James Clear says it beautifully, and let me paraphrase it for you:

*"The problem with smart people is they can come up with a good reason for not doing anything. They are smart enough to find the cracks, to foresee the challenges, and to talk themselves out of the idea. They are experts at justifying their lack of courage or lack of action with an intelligent excuse.*

*But there will always be reasons to not do something, and this is particularly true of anything worth doing. We value those moments in which we overcame our challenge, not those in which we avoided it. Ultimately, action is a choice. The choice to emphasize the reasons for doing it despite the reasons you have for avoiding it."*

Bro, and you know, CA students are smart as hell!

One of this smartness came to surface when we realised one chapter, called Activity Based Costing was transferred from CA Final syllabus to CA-Intermediate syllabus.

If Costing as a subject was not enough, now making a CPT-cleared-student deal with a chapter of CA Final was another thing!

Let me tell you, my fear (and our collective group fear) made it bigger than we thought.

There would be a reason why a chapter was moved from one level to another. We were not babies to understand that. But maybe the babies inside all of us hadn't grown up :)

More so, people designing the curriculum are all Chartered Accountants.

If that was not enough and we were screwed, we were all screwed together. No one had it easier if it was not easy in the first place!

Like James said, there will always be reasons to not do something, and this is true of anything worth doing.

Maybe we should rather focus on action, because ultimately action is a choice. Because maybe the reasons for doing the thing are (and should) weigh our circumstances.

**Maybe we are all bigger than we think.**

**Maybe we shrink ourselves so smaller than what we are all capable of.**

**Maybe we all have it in us, even when we can't see it. The precise time when we must see it.**

# Chapter 13

# Can We Skip to the Good Part?

Okay, I know I have shared a lot about what did not work out.

I'll take a moment to share what did work out.

Section 8 of the Companies Act is a section that defines companies with charitable goals. However, ICAI in its suggested answers would mention the word as charitable "objects". So each time one would need notes or help from another student, the other would say: "Why are you asking me, am I Section 8?"

Or the power of consistency.

During the hours after evening lectures, my friend Harshita (yes, the same one, who is now a Chartered Accountant) and I would sit back after the class, and we made it a rule of thumb to revise sections, numericals and accounting and auditing standards.

Even in CPT, I had a study buddy called Karuna Tolani with whom I would revise lessons after classes got over. We cleared CPT together, however, just like me, she has moved on to pursue other projects that she absolutely loves.

When the Inter result did come, the power of consistency also showed its magic.

While almost everyone around me easily secured 60+ marks, I got a decent 55. Not bad, huh.

With Law, I made a grave mistake of studying only the notes. Not the book.

For Costing, maybe I had disqualified myself even before I started. You know how.

For Taxation, I can now compute your taxable income. Better late than never :)

So yes, there were (and still are) some beautiful pieces of journey that you want to take with yourself.

However, a journey is the one that always continues. So will we…

# Chapter 14

# One for Health, One for Wealth

After I gave the May 2018 exam for Inter, my parents and I visited my sister in London in July 2018.

She was studying physiotherapy there. We went there to meet her, and also spend some family time together.

While my Dad's older daughter was learning how to relieve people of their unwanted body pressure, his younger daughter was taking an unwanted mental pressure.

This time, my mental pressure was a visualisation, where my father would introduce both of us sisters to a distant uncle as: "Hey, meet my two daughters. One for health and one for wealth."

This was also the month when my results of the May 2018 attempt would loom.

With this mental pressure, also came the creeping realisation of not giving my best. The inner truth of messing up already.

The instinct of being aware that you are not what everyone thinks you are.

But a part of me also had the tiniest sliver of hope, that maybe if I secured 200 in the first group, a borderline pass mark, I might still inch closer to my visualisation.

You see, all these Olympic athletes and professional sports players are visualising all of the time.

I was also watching a lot of reaction videos of people, especially the ones who did clear Inter in the first attempt.

So visualisation was top notch. But I had forgotten just one thing.

***The professional athletes who practice visualization are also preparing at the***

***highest level in the world. They are not doubting themselves, they are not mailing it in, they are exceeding the standards of preparation they set for themselves, they are not giving anything less than their 100%.***

Visualization works like a charm when you have the preparation right.

Anyway, while we were on the famous "hop on hop off London bus" the results were announced. For some reason, the results site was not loading on our phones. So I called up a friend in India to check my result.

When he did, he asked me to hand over my phone to my sister. My heart dropped a beat.

My sister knew. I knew. We all knew. Maybe I knew already.

But a last hopeful ray within me asked her: "First group to hua hoga (I would have at least cleared the first group.)"

Nope.

I still have no idea what made me ask that question. A part of me already knew the answer.

Maybe the same part of me was looking for a hope, a reason to persist when I knew I didn't have any.

Anyway, I started crying instantly. Uncontrollably. It was my first ever Facetime with failure.

I am glad my family was around me at the time. My Mom was consoling me. My Dad was very calm, because he has a famous saying to his aid: Success lies everywhere, not only in exams. My sister tried fun ways to distract me by making me think of something else other than exams or CA, just to elevate my mood.

As I pause for a moment to think about my sister, she is my biggest cheerleader. Not only that, if only I had 10% of her courage and 10% of her ability to ignore what other people say, my life would be sorted. Maybe starting from the first year of this half decade I spent wandering. Though she is a physiotherapist by profession, she is my psychologist, my personal doctor on call, and my helpline whenever I need her. And since she is my unpaid therapist, she ensures I do her silly tasks in lieu of monetary compensation I didn't pay her.

*When God (and Santa Claus) couldn't be everywhere, they created siblings.*

Anyhow, the day of the results was itself weird.

It was my first international trip where I was in my senses.

I had travelled to Hong Kong before, but I barely remembered anything. So I was anyway adopting to the new culture.

I am an Indian, that too from Mumbai. We have no concept of winters. And here I was, in the cold and chilly London in my jacket and hood, while it was a heatwave for the natives :) And then, this news.

Too much internal and external chaos. Too little familiarity. Humans contempt newness anyway.

The days that followed weren't brighter either.

I was coping with the first ever failure of my life.

A part of me was also feeling silently betrayed—this is where you land up when you don't want to do the thing you are doing in the first place. Worse, I didn't even know back then that I didn't want this career choice for myself.

Had this been something I loved or was enthused about, I would have figured a way from facing failure anyway.

I also saw my friends filing the form for articleship, the one you are eligible to file only if you clear the first Group of Inter.

But the good part is I did not question my abilities at this point. One failure in this journey was fine.

I eventually got to a point of telling myself:

If at all there was a movie made on my story, this journey from the downfall to the top rising like a phoenix would be worth the watch.

I don't know if a movie is still on the cards, but a book definitely is, in your palms :) Oh, so is another failure :))

# Chapter 15

# I Am a Failure, and This is My Story

We returned from London a month later, on 17th August, 2018. I was now fresh, and excited to start studying again.

However, it did not feel very nice to study the same books and notes again.

I am someone who believes proper stationery (e.g., highlighter) equips you with the right focus on your studies. But my books have markings already! I did not know where to use the highlighter and red pens now.

But the show must go on. So did the studies.

However, I have to admit at times I would lock up my room and cry looking at the books. Each chapter, each question has a memory at some point in the classroom with your batchmates. The same batchmates, a lot of whom were seniors now.

Three months later, the second attempt of Inter and my semester-end B.Com exams would overlap. Even though it was "just one" exam, the emotional mess that causes overlapping exams was good enough to mess things up. There is perhaps a reason the world rewards focus and makes us pay the price for multitasking.

By far, I was not a wise nut at prioritization.

So, I took up the Herculean task of appearing in both groups of Inter, along with B.Com. This was a drastic mistake, because I had not studied well for the second group in the first attempt itself. In this second attempt as well, I started studying right away without even being aware of the syllabus.

The result had to come back to bite me. It did.

Of course, I cried.

I improved my score from the last time. I also secured 53 marks in Taxation which was a huge leap from 39 in the previous one. But I still couldn't get through the minimum passing marks. In life, you do not get step-marking.

# Chapter 16

# Late Does Not Mean Laid-back

Now I am gearing up for the next attempt, my third attempt, which is the May 2019 attempt.

My peers suggested I take up one group at a time, but being a rebel is sometimes a curse than a choice. Like it turned out for me.

However, I have now started studying rigorously. And now the exams were delayed, because of the Central Assembly elections in May 2019.

With the delay, my mood for studies also vanished.

As if that rigorous study could take me through, and my November 2018 failure was solely due to my mood taking off!

Anyway, most peers were my juniors now, and it felt pathetic to share the same shoes as them.

My best friend, Megha, took friendship for real. She would come and help me with advanced accounts while pursuing her articleship. I thank my stars for her, literally.

Remember how in school and college your authority increases with growing age and class?

CA failure humbles you in that way. One day you are with your friends, a few months later your friends are ahead of you, another few months later you are a peer of your juniors, and if you were as unlucky as I happened to be, sometimes your juniors go on to become your seniors.

Anyway, one of those days my juniors were discussing how to memorise perquisites, and all I could hear was parasites.

I felt like a parasite. The feeling of being stuck in the same place forever.

(For the uninitiated, perquisites refer to the benefits or perks that an employee receives in addition to their regular salary or wages. These are non-cash benefits that can be taxable under the head of "Income from Salaries" as per the income tax laws in many countries, including India.)

Anyway, as is characteristically me, not listening to anyone including myself, I went on to appear for both groups.

Cherry on the cake, ICAI had now introduced the MCQ pattern in the exam. So what MCQs for practice were limited and went live on the ICAI portal pretty late. Drishti loves change :) She is a pro at managing it :))

The worst part, I was studying by myself this time, sans any coaching, so I had no way of understanding how to get to the answers, even though the answers were right in front of me!

By this time google drive and pen drive lectures were also not that well-known, as they gathered momentum around the Covid pandemic.

I felt lost.

This was also the time when it was easy to solve the questions in a subjective format. As much as it was not useful anymore, it was an important validation. That I was not dumb at concepts, just that I was unable to cope with the change as well as FOMO where I was actually missing out!

Sometimes, looking back, sitting on a raised platform in my room, with my diary, writing or finger painting, at other times with a coffee on the Marine Drive, or simply thinking while munching cashews and almonds, I wonder how much of myself I had lost in the process.

I am basically a positive person. I do not wait for anyone to show me the way. I create mine. I do that as a habit, as a lifestyle.

And here I was, downplaying myself through excuses for not surviving, whereas others were thriving.

*One of my constant and biggest life lessons is that not everything is for everyone. As pessimistic as it may sound, nothing is more optimistic than that.*

*If you expect Neeraj Chopra to score runs like Virat Kohli, you are doing them both a disservice.*

*Or, if you expect Roger Federer to swim like Michale Phelps, you aren't doing them anything better instead.*

*Or expect Jennifer Aniston to play a role that is a fit for Courteney Cox…well, you know.*

And here we are, or at least I was, expecting failure in one area to extrapolate to calling myself a failure. If that was not enough, I stayed at it for 6 years, of which 5 years were dwindling and drowning in failures.

Sometimes we become our biggest enemies, hoping for a change without changing anything.

However, the pressure of the third attempt had crept in. Loud and clear. If that was not enough, the friends of mine who had now cleared the exam and were in CA Final, kept saying "CA Inter was nothing. CA Final is a demon."

Yeah, CA Inter was nothing. Which is why I couldn't clear it in the first place!

Anyhow, we give the exams. I would have an upset stomach in the morning, cold feet, anything that is a form of not being at one with yourself.

After the exams, I attended the Tarang Fest organised by Bombay Chartered Accountants Society. BCAS, as they call it. Got exposed to industry practitioners. Seniors. And big names in the industry.

And I have nothing to answer the questions seniors asked: "Which firm are you pursuing your articleship from?" Because I haven't cleared my Inter yet.

I felt very low that time.

While I don't feel the same emotion anymore, and have learnt to keep a badge of humour next to my failures, take it from me if you are ever feeling low: you need to feel low for the crimes you commit. Nothing, absolutely nothing else. Got it?

On that note, it is time we go to the result of the May 2019 attempt.

# Chapter 17

# May 19 to November 19

This was the time I was strongly considering quitting.

By this time I have also become an active member of the Tarang fest of BCAS, because I love volunteering. It is held every year in June. This way, the people who gave their exams in May could attend it. And, the people who have their exams in November could also attend it without the anxiety of exam preparation.

For the uninitiated, I have never feared approaching people. Thus, as a CA student, I would speak to everyone in the committee, whether it is a new person or a past member. I also have a habit of voluntarily taking up work and finishing it really well. This is something that was noticed by the HR committee at Tarang. Hence, they made me an active member of the committee. I would give my opinions, draft scripts, and manage things when I saw mismanagement. A simple example of how good I was at certain things, yet completely blinded by my own self-created aspirations. Or delusions.

However, over time, I spoke to people, connected with seniors, got myself some counselling, and all of those conversations told me that it was normal to fail in CA. We even had a running joke in the BCAS office during Tarang: If someone cleared CA in the first attempt, it means they haven't covered the entire syllabus lol.

Sorry CAs. Just joking, if you know you know!!

Anyway, after the Tarang fest in June 2019, I studied for the 3 months remaining before the November 2019 exam. Let's be honest, not all 3 months. In July 2019, I went on a budget trip to Amsterdam and Paris with my elder sister. We went there with our savings, living in hostels, having cooked food in AirBnbs, walking on foot in Amsterdam. We learnt a great deal about each other. We confessed how much we missed each other.

I was someone who was voluntarily picking up work at fests and doing it well, and was also procrastinating on studying for the toughest examination, which was also my 4$^{th}$ attempt. It clearly showed not my lack of sincerity but my lack of interest and joy. Something I wish I could listen to more.

This time, I also studied with all the irritation and frustration.

You know, how some conversations put an end to your anxiety and make you feel home, right?

I did not feel any of those after having all the counselling I had, that made me reconsider staying in CA. Maybe it was a bandage at best, but did not truly truly convince me to continue being in CA. What it indeed did, was maybe make me spend a couple of more years trying and trying and trying, when I did not want to do it in the first place.

There is a zeal, a determination, a rigour of persisting, especially when you want to do something. At this point, I did not want to. I am not guilty about it. If you have a very strong inner feeling and have it more often, it is your divine responsibility to honour it, instead of shutting it down.

*My recurring feeling had now changed from "Drishti CA se nikal" to "Drishti CA ko nikaal". Translated: (Drishti, get out of CA course asap to get through CA course asap.)*

I tried not listening to it for the longest time, as my mind had also gone on to race to Plan B now.

Anyway, Drishti still being the old Drishti, I took fastrack lectures of practical subjects and to get a hang of concepts. It had already been 2 years since I had ever understood a concept from scratch! The doubt had started taking the space where understanding used to occupy a headspace.

November attempt of CA exams also collides with Diwali. And more often than not, you tend to miss out on the festival.

But hey, I love Diwali! I love filling in the bonus envelopes of the staff at Dad's office, writing their names, and out of habit drawing a smiley next to them. I missed doing it this time. I skipped going to Dad's office entirely, for the celebrations! Even though the staff understood, they inquired Dad about my CA status.

Anyway, after the November 2019 attempt, I did something for the very first time.

# Chapter 18

# I Walked Barefoot to Mata Vaishno Devi

Post my November 2019 exams, I walked barefoot to Mata Vaishno Devi.

Well, not barefoot from Mumbai to Mata Vaishno Devi. Rather barefoot from the point you begin the journey of the ascent to the temple. It was November cold. Barefeet is not super cool. The weather wasn't bad per se, it was manageable. Plus, if you are walking for so long, your body generates a lot of body heat.

I know like I know like I know that there is a superpower or energy.

A part of me knows that when a human being is sick and tired of being sick and tired of their problems, they remember God wholeheartedly.

Which is what I did.

I don't believe God can do everything. However, I do believe that God guides us towards the right direction, so we can make our own decisions.

But let me tell you, I still "knew" something was off. The heart knew, the mind still hadn't given up, though.

Eventually, when the results did come in January 2020, I did not clear the exams.

I was also about to give 6th and final semester exams of B.Com in (which month?). But there was no way I would give up my CA dream. (*My* dream?) I was also confused about what to pursue after graduation— should I study the same books I have been studying for almost 3 years now?

However, very soon, two months later, the pandemic hit. And we were all thinning about survival.

If I pause sometimes to think about it, it hits me like a lightning bolt:

I am sure there were students who worked harder and smarter than me, those who, while making sacrifices on Diwali like me, had prepared for the syllabus much in advance, who had acute clarity of their concepts; and I still think some might have failed.

While clearing CA exam is also partly a matter of luck and how many percentage of students ICAI wants to pass, I also think that the ones who get through have two things in common:

1.  They want it badly. (Did I?)

2.  They work hard with a strategy, and are also street smart outside of being book smart. (I am street smart, but I'd know people who work very hard in silos that eventually make the results tick in their favour.)

As I reflect on my favourite platform at home, I realise Mata Vaishno Devi was in favour of those who ticked both these boxes. And she helped me in a bigger way, by nudging me eventually towards the right decision of quitting CA.

*Remember that God does not do things for you but guides you?*

*And if you do not get what you asked for, something better is always there. Always.*

But before that, I must share the story of the pandemic within me, along with the pandemic that was waiting for all of us the world over…

# Chapter 19

# I Felt a Pandemic Within Me

In January 2020, much before the Coronavirus became a pandemic in March 2020, I became a student coordinator at the BCAS.

BCAS, or the Bombay Chartered Accountants Society, is a voluntary professional organisation consistently oriented towards knowledge, ethics and community, dedicated to professional development of Chartered Accountants.

There are multiple committees in BCAS, where speaker sessions, seminars, events are held.

After noticing my work in 2019, the Human Resource Development Committee and the former student co-ordinators nominated my name for the student co-ordinator of Tarang in 2020.

Thus, I along with other members of the BCAS started preparing for the Tarang Fest 2020.

Tarang is a CA students' annual day—it is a fest and a college environment which the CA students missed while pursuing CA. We have different competitions— ranging from debates, essay writing, talk hawk, talent show, antakshari, drawing, quiz, and what not!

However, when the lockdown started in March 2020, we by default moved to creating campaigns and spreading awareness about Trang on social media.

We reached out to CA pages on Instagram, and requested them to post a post and a story to promote Tarang. We also convinced them to do it pro-bono. And they did!

This way, we reached out to CA students pan-India, not just Mumbai, in a short span of time.

This was also the time I started getting a lot of fame and recognition through what I was doing. Fame not as in that I was being papped at the airport (it is another thing that the flights were not operational anyway). Fame as in members and students in BCAS were now recognising me. I was also being recognised in other CA circles, such as WICASA, which is Western India Chartered Accountants Students Association (WICASA) is the student wing of Western India Regional Council of Institute of Chartered Accountants Association (WIRC-ICAI).

***This also acted as a lure, another sticking point for me to not quit CA.***

I believe when you have made all the effort and almost decided that you want to quit, something will fall into place to trick you into believing you shouldn't. Me falling into place in BCAS was exactly that. It almost bribed me into giving more into CA, when I perhaps had nothing to give.

Anyway, like everything offline being postponed, so did CA exams.

I was not sure if it was a good sign, or was it finally the time to bid adieu to CA? Anyhow, with uncertainty all around, I kept preparing with inconsistency.

My B.Com final semester exams were also postponed. They were finally held online in October the same year.

Frustrated and flustered, I was also not able to spend some quality time with my family, now that every single one was at home all of the time.

However, the truth is that the vaccine was still far away. At least not for a year. I remember it was first available in September of 2021. Before it was finally available, it was only a matter of if and when, and dealing with the external uncertainty and the self-created anxiety.

The May 2020 exam was postponed due to the pandemic already.

Finally, after multiple postponements, the ICAI finally decided to conduct the November 2020 exams. The institute also gave an option of "opt-out", which meant that the students whose exams were due in May (and now November) 2020 could opt out of the exams, and finally appear in January 2021, and it won't be counted as "another attempt".

This was ICAI's way of ensuring that we could choose our safety, as well as it won't tarnish our attempts, which is something we all carry all our lives. I thought it was a welcome move.

It was also a lucrative deal to buy more time and not add up additional CA attempts on my resume.

# Chapter 20

# This Time, I Gave Everything I Had

I finally took the much-delayed May 2020 exam, that was delayed to November 2020, that I chose to opt out of; and chose to appear for the January 2021 exam.

This time, I gave everything I could.

For some change, I moved to Dad's Bua's home (Kanta Bua) in Khar.

It might come across as a rude statement to say, but my family always has some work for me at any damn time of the day. My home, like most Indian homes, has some sort of buzz going on at all times. Which is quite disturbing when you are wanting to study with focus.

With Bua's home and only Dad's Bua and Uncle staying there, I had an environment of much-needed focus.

I could get an entire place to myself.

Bua is also someone who is chilled out by nature. One of those positive people who has changed herself with time. Her house is what I call "my soulhouse". She lives her entire day with discipline, has a routine aligned to her days, and also has food on time, that too the right food :)

Also her two kids were married by now.

Since I also enjoy the atmosphere there, I was quite comfortable there. I even appeared for exams while staying there.

When I appeared for my exams from her place, I could actually feel that I was appearing for exams with a calm state of mind.

Eventually, I secured 358 marks out of 800, whereas the minimum passing marks were 400.

I still failed short of at least 5 marks per subject, and an aggregate of 50% marks. But I could not have done anything else! I really couldn't!

I had revision lectures downloaded on my phone. I would listen to them while walking/sleeping or when I was extremely tired of reading the notes.

I even had consistent dreams of entering the exam hall with a calculator in my hand.

I gave test series and even appeared in mock examinations, securing well enough to be certain that I would clear exams this time.

But I remember I messed up miserably in the Taxation exam. I even failed to keep up with the amendments. Even changed a few of my teachers.

*Looking back, I realise you must stay true to a teacher you believe in or pick a teacher that your gut feeling says, and close all other new options that keep coming. I feel sad to say this but a lot of market leading faculties are in the business of luring well-meaning students like me who were stuck in a consistent failure loop, and would succumb to the next available option.*

"Is baar 400 paar" OR "Where there is a will, there is a way; after every November, there is a May" were the consistent slogans that the market was abuzz with.

As funny as they sounded, they were not funny! When you go through exactly the same situation, it breaks your heart.

Anyhow, we now know the result.

Before we go on to what happened in the next attempt, I do want to share a bit about what my family could have done.

# Chapter 21

# I Wish My Family Was More Supportive

A lot of people struggle to get family support even though there is financial support, and that is something I do want to voice my opinions on.

*I also want to do this because sometimes in order for your own family to win, the elders in the family need to draw some boundaries, which, unfortunately a lot of Indian families struggle with.*

My family is no different.

I know my family has been supportive of me in my journey, but being supportive isn't good enough, especially if the mountain is as big as a CA exam.

The discipline required is exponential, sacrifices are plenty, and anyone who truly truly wants to succeed needs to learn to say no a lot more often. I genuinely feel my parents could have taken the baton in their hands when it came to relatives, and asked them to "not enter" our house till the time my CA exams were done.

But they were given the treatment of just normal exams!

Not on purpose, but they perhaps thought that this won't make much of a difference.

I also wish my father sat down with me and we chalked out a plan that I could adhere to.

Our household had things going on at random, no fixed time for meals; and since my father has a business of his own, there was no fixed time of his returning home.

All of this left a huge impact in my head. I think it was impacting me since the very beginning, but now that I had given 5 attempts already, I could now see that some things were amiss from the start.

I do think with a specific plan of action, I would have cleared my exams.

After all, all the students who do clear their exams, especially the ones who do it in the first two attempts have just one thing in common. Planning followed by relentless execution.

For you to plan better, I am sharing a QR code. Use a scanner from your smart phone, once you scan, download the file, you will have access to a vision board, to- do list and an undated monthly calender. Take a print, keep it accessible on your study desk at all times.

*Here's the QR code:*

**Without a plan, I was executing only based on my wishful thinking. Wishful thinking rarely makes your wishes come true.**

I definitely needed an accountability partner, someone who would keep me on my toes, and who would not dare mail it in, and expect serious commitment, consistency and execution from me.

My Mom was busy taking care of home and grandparents, and my father was taking care of business. My sister had started working at a physiotherapy clinic in Mumbai.

I also tried bringing these things to their notice but nothing changed.

Human beings as a species hate change. They change only when there is a strong enough reason from within, and for parents, their kid (that too the younger one) asking them to change is not a strong enough reason. They will love you unconditionally, that is for sure. However, somehow a lot of parents forget to think that their kid is not always a toddler, and has their own needs as well. Especially if they are emotional needs, maybe our parents collectively could do a slightly better job.

As these reflections continued dawning on me, my interest in CA continued dwindling.

# Chapter 22

# I Skipped the Next Attempt

After January 2021, the next attempt was in July 2021.

Usually, the CA attempts used to be in May and November of each year, however, because November 2020 was an attempt most people could opt out of due to COVID, its eventual exam was held in January 2021, the one that I appeared in.

Now the next attempt was in July primarily due to the second wave of COVID, that had engulfed India in late April–May 2021.

It was more devastating than the first wave, and was something that even our family couldn't escape this time.

Before we get there, I'd take a moment to explain my headspace during those 6 months.

Now I was not mentally ready to appear for the exam. Like you would feel sometimes in school days that you wish you had a fracture so you could not appear for an exam that was supposed to be held the next day, I felt exactly the same.

***I had mentally resigned.***

I also gave away all my books and enrolled for ACCA.

Like CA, this was again not an academically thought-out decision, it was perhaps an emotional decision to still have a professional degree. If not CA, ACCA; I thought.

But eventually I did not end up doing ACCA, because studying the content gave me deja-vu vibes of some of the CA Inter syllabus.

Also, in April of 2021, the whole of India was engulfed in the second wave of Covid. Mumbai was one of the most affected cities.

My Mom was one of those affected. She was admitted in the Covid centre, and in home isolation before that. All of us as a family unit were now coming together to hold the fort. When it is a question of survival of your family, you are obviously not thinking about your career.

However, when things did get better, in June 2021, I took a remote entrepreneurial edge program from a mentor of the London School of Business. For some reason, I made an epic presentation on that course.

Still, somehow, I wanted to drag on to the CA course, whereas my actions were clearly aligned towards so much more and different.

What is wrong with me?

I'm also thinking exactly that.

# Chapter 23

# I Lost My Baba

On the night of 21st September 2021, we lost the rock of our house.

Baba or Sandy, as we would call our grandfather, passed away on a day that he lived fully well.

He was healthy by all standards. No recent health complaints.

Very particular of his regiment towards his body and his entire schedule, he would follow routines during the day to the T. He was the epitome of discipline when it came to his health and commitments.

The day he passed away, he went for his morning walk as usual, and returned with fresh fruits and vegetables. Then loaded the refrigerator with his shopping. After having a usual day, he went into his room after dinner and started watching Pakistani tales on YouTube.

After that, we never saw him.

It turns out, his room's door was open when my Mom saw him lying on the bed, vomited on one side and urinated on the other. My mom screamed at what she saw and in less than a second, my sister and I, and our neighbours were there.

He was cold and unconscious.

We checked his sugar, blood pressure, but no response. We rubbed his feet, my sister tried giving him CPR but nothing worked. (My sister is a physiotherapist, thank god!)

One of our neighbours who also happens to be my Dad's friend, Ravi Uncle, helped us rush Baba to the nearby hospital, without wasting any more time. My sister drove Baba to the hospital, along with our Mom and Ravi uncle. I was at home with my grandmother. Before my sister and Mom could even admit him, a doctor came near their car and declared our Baba was no more.

But this wasn't it. We still had to break the worst news of his lifetime to our father, who was at his construction site office, in a meeting. Since all of us were still reeling with shock, Ravi Uncle came to aid again. He gathered the courage to call him, and asked him to leave immediately. Dad did suspect something was terribly wrong, but we did not want him to go through it alone, so we did not break the reason.

When he did arrive, it was a heart-shattering moment, to say the least, to see my father shattered, crying uncontrollably, to see his father not responding.

It was a shock for all of us. But one of the things I did not recognize back then but am in admiration of was how my Mom was strong like a rock and stood up to take care of the entire family..

My mom was all determined to handle dad's reactions and made him face the situation boldly. Her parents, my maternal grandparents, passed away a few years ago. Which is what perhaps gave my Mom the much-needed courage we as a family needed.

As relatives would come over, Mom would attend to them, not bother dad much. She was also the one who took care of all the rituals with the help of relatives and neighbours.

During this time, my sister's marriage conversations were at peak. My sister's then friend, Amit, went on to become her husband because Baba convinced our father about him. He was also the one who lobbied for them to go to the US for their career choices. My father never saw this side of Baba. But here he was, modern and adapting himself to changing times.

My sister and I would openly share things with Baba and not with dad. The entire day in our house, we would have light moments of banter with Baba and as soon as dad was home, we went back to our routine tasks. Not that dad was too strict but simply because Baba was very chill. As granddaughters we enjoyed every bit of occasions, daytime gossip, evening snacks, we quite lived a life.

*Whenever we used to shop, we would show our dresses to Baba and he would make faces and ask, "where will you wear this? Now for you to wear this dress, I will have to throw a party," then give a hearty*

*laugh and say in sindhi, "Chhokar pagal aahe tu!"*
*(Translated: (lovingly) you mad girl!)*

As I think about my Baba, it was him who shaped my sister and I into bold and confident human beings. He would pick us up from the school bus every day at 3.20 pm without fail, despite the scorching Mumbai heat. He was our helpline for every single thing. We both would have blue lays only when he got it for us, no other time. I not only believe, I know that the blue lays he got us had a completely different taste altogether. Till date, that packet reminds us of him. Needless to say, we have almost stopped having it. It just doesn't taste like that anymore.

Even though ours was a conventional middle-class family, he happily changed rules for both me and my sister, without either of us asking. We could attend college parties, bring home male friends, go out for dinners, and even go for overnight trips (with proper tour guides of course). In most families what is considered as a taboo, he was the one who made it normal for us. Of course, he ensured our safety first, and then allowed us to be merry our way. A subtle yet strong way of how one should be: hard outside but soft on the inside.

After Baba passed away, I reflect on life and its fragility often.

There are days you wake up and you decide you will take charge of your entire day. You have your day planned to the T, on how you want it to go. And then something unexpected happens on one of the "normal" days and you remember those scenes and the exact spots in your home where that happened, and the memories shatter you forever.

But the sad, even though unwanted realisation of life is that you have to learn to live with the grief and find happiness. You don't dismiss the grief and the emptiness, you manage to be happy despite it. This is what Baba would have wanted for us. This is what he would have been proud to see us doing: living our lives to the fullest.

I hope, I truly hope he is proud of the individual I am turning to be.

In the journey of failures, I have been through in my academic life, you might want to ask how this instance fits the entire scheme of things.

And I want to say it does.

The death of a family member, especially someone who lived in the same house that you did, who shaped you up so much as an individual, is not a small thing. If anything, it is one of the 5 lowest moments of your life ever.

You know by now how much I was struggling with CA exam results. It was an emotionally draining journey. So was this loss in the family. Loss of your rock. Loss of your Big Parent, the parent of your parents, who would root for you when your parents would make sure you were disciplined.

Regardless of the fact that if I appeared in the coming November exam or whatever I did next in life, some voids cannot be avoided. You must feel them fully in order to deal with them.

I could have easily continued through the book pretending nothing had happened.

But till when we as a society will continue brushing away our emotional wounds as if nothing happened?

Even though I could not control my Dada's passing away, I must allow the pain to visit, so it does not get compressed within me, only to pop out as anger, quietness, resentment and its cousins, later on.

This bit was a failure that I had no hand in. But it did have a hand in my life. And for that, I wear it with pride and honour, not hide it with wail and horror.

The year wasn't the most beautiful one—my career and random choices, Mom's health, and then Baba passing away. But sometimes you need a bad year to make important life choices. I think I made a lot of those in that year. In a way, all of this quietly nudged me to eventually quit CA a year after Baba's demise.

So even if 2021 was a year where I did not "accomplish" much, a lot of losses brought about some priceless life lessons.

# Chapter 24

# Relevance and Irrelevance

The next attempt, that happened in December 2021.

The delayed November 2020 attempt happened in January 2021, because of which the May attempt happened in July 2021. Thus, leading to the November attempt being postponed to December 2021.

After a year that made me reflect a lot on life as well as career, I still wasn't in a place to "try once more and see what happens".

Also, with not even 3 months to Dada's passing, I wasn't in much of a mindspace to dabble with the idea of convincing myself.

The next month, January 2022, was also when my sister got married. Baba was the most excited about her wedding, but life had other plans. The celebrations were limited due to covid restrictions, but we had unlimited fun.

However, in order to stay relevant and tell myself that I was doing "something" I started pursuing M.Com.

But now I think it was a wise decision to do that. Not because pursuing M.Com. would change anything in my career trajectory, but because my personal value at the time was to keep moving forward and not sit idle.

You cannot just measure the relevance of something in terms of direct returns. Sometimes the return is indirect and intangible, and in my case, what M.Com. gave me was the tag that "I am not wasting my time". And the fact that I am a postgraduate for life :)

Anyhow, as the next attempt of May 2022 started inching closer, I also started feeling a void within me.

The guilt of leaving a course midway.

The frustration of quitting. (Remember the old line: "Winners don't quit and quitters don't win"?)

The constantly piling up irritation.

I would avoid speaking to people who would constantly ask what I was doing. I was skipping dinner invites or meeting relatives.

My mind had constant thoughts:

*Was taking breaks from attempts helping me, or was I just wasting my time, when it could have been the attempt that I could pass?*

*Ah, the mind. The messy man's mind — that makes you believe all the could have, should have, would have and makes you the culprit.*

The same messed up mind that made me continue overthinking even during the May 2022 exams I appeared for.

I made my stellar mistake of doing both groups together, one more time again. Appearing through exams with racing thoughts of what could have gone right, this time I failed badly.

While I did appear for the exam with good intent, in CA exams, planning and preparation often hold more weight than intent. But I was already not in the groove of studying. Even though I had resumed after a break, I still wonder if that break was something I should have finally broken up my relationship with CA.

But I also think we humans have a tendency to give ourselves one more, just one more chance. Just in case this time things come together…

It is so easy for me to sit where I am right now and blame myself that I could have given up earlier.

But every single one of us has a resistance ratio, post which they give up.

During all the failed attempts and all the what-if's that don't work out, "what if this time it works out" keeps all of us afloat.

We learn all our much-needed lessons there, if we are not able to stay afloat.

And then when we finally make the move, we do it forever and ever and ever. With zero regrets.

Only courage and pride that we did try and give our best.

And then learn all the lessons to put it into a book that we would wear as a badge of honour forever and ever and ever :)

But, I think you gotta listen to the story of "my last and final attempt". Ever.

# Chapter 25

# The Friendships That Were Not Meant to Be, the Nos That Were Left Unsaid

A lot of people who are in the stage that I was once at, might be going through this. We want to hang around with our friends.

We want to attend that dinner party.

We want to not say no to that weekend getaway.

We think we might lose our friends if we don't get out with them.

I think they are not our friends in the first place if our friendship is determined by hanging around with them. And not by focusing on our careers at the moment.

The real friends stay no matter what.

We tend to think a lot about lost friendships. Especially like the above ones. It feels bad at the moment when we sacrifice.

However, the cycle of May to November is tedious. You cannot hold the fort and hold fake friends as well. Yes, it does create a void. There were a few friendships that grew apart.

Thus, now I have become very picky about the people I allow into my life. I am not labelling all that happened as beautiful or brutal, just that it is.

You are not prepared for it, but you gotta accept that you have to deal with it in the middle of the mess of your career, and figure your way through it.

So is the case with saying no. The two-letter powerful word.

When you are focused on achieving something, you gotta say no to everything else. Unfortunately, a lot of us would prefer giving in instead of saying no. The two-letter powerful word isn't a part of our upbringing.

So, when my parents would receive a party invite when I was in the peak of my study periods, I could not say no, because, hey, I don't know how to say it. So couldn't my parents say a no, because they didn't know it either.

*In the journey of saying yes to everyone, sometimes you forget to say yes to the most important person: yourself.*

*But life happens, as I have noticed.*

*You learn. You get better. You move on. But to move on, you must reflect on what all happened. Which is what I have attempted to do here :)*

# Chapter 26

# The Need to Draw Our Boundaries

One of the things I absolutely love is to decorate the food I am eating.

A good presentation is basically my P0, or my number one priority, as we call it.

Thus, when we have relatives over, I am at my absolute best preparation for them as well.

Yes, we are a typical Indian family that keeps having relatives over :)

Anyhow, one fine day I had prepared a healthy chaat. Not the calorie counter that you get in Chowpatty in Mumbai, but a healthier version. Garnished it with quinoa, moong and some basic garnishing of onion, tomato, salt, pepper, chilli flakes and coriander leaves.

*While relishing it, my uncle passed a comment, perhaps in a jiffy "You cook so well, you could have done something in culinary." That comment pierced through me like a bullet through a glass.*

*It was not a compliment. He was quietly mocking my CA journey. I thought people had moved on. Just like I had.*

*Truth be told, that comment messed up my head. I almost thought I should learn how to be ruthless and answer him back. But it wasn't worth it.*

I also thought that had I become a CA, he would not make this kind of distasteful remark on what I should do.

I wish my close ones understood this.

But I also think that people who have an unending nerve to wreck, they will figure out a way to do it.

Even if I had become a CA. Even if I had become the President of the Institute of Chartered Accountants of India. Even if I had become the President of India.

The best lesson I could learn from this is, to develop a thick inner skin, that the comments of "family" and naysayers did not affect me.

And to always cook for people who truly enjoy your company. Not everyone is worth you :)

You do you. You cannot make everyone happy.

When the wrong people won't get the adequate masalas to feed their ego and soul, they generally walk away.

Mind your own business and take care of your health.

I disturbed myself emotionally for the longest time because of these failures in CA. As I reflect, it was merely a stupid decision to weigh people's opinions in my head all the time.

A person gets tired due to mental garbage not due to physical strain.

# Chapter 27

# The Last One

Before the results for the May exam arrived, I casually bumped into a counsellor's profile on LinkedIn. A CA herself, Riddhi, was mentoring ACCA students.

Well, ACCA is something I enrolled for early in 2021, but the events of 2021 did not make me consider it seriously.

Now I was. In part, because I was seriously considering letting go of CA. In part, because I still wanted a professional degree. Higher education does have some beautiful benefits, one of which being hanging around with other smart people.

Anyhow, I spoke to her to understand more about ACCA, and if she would help me as a teacher during my ACCA exams.

But counsellors are smart people. So was mine.

She suggested before going ahead with teaching, I needed counselling, on what I truly wanted.

During our conversations, she rightly pointed out that I was attached more to CA, and pursuing ACCA would only complicate things further. It is strange she pointed that out, because while studying for ACCA, I did have a deja-vu of the CA syllabus.

Anyhow, she suggested this time, in November 2022, I appear for CA with proper planning and appear for only the first group, helped me create a study plan, and even took my mock tests for the exam.

This was the first time I appeared for the first group.

I also told myself that if I did not clear the exam this time, I would be done with the CA course forever. I would not continue any further.

*It was finally a now-or-never moment.*

*When the result finally did arrive, I cried. The last time.*

Not because I did not clear the exam. Somehow I knew it already. But because now I knew I would never ever become a CA.

Because at this moment, the effort of those 5 years would become a sunk cost. Because I would also not be able to do ACCA because it would give me high deja-vu feelings of the CA course.

I have a long life ahead, and I know things will eventually fall in place.

But I also have no regrets of crying for the last time. It's good to use those tears as fuel for your journey forward.

# Chapter 28

# What the Teachers Say

Before we move on to talk about how life eventually unfolded for me, I want to take a moment to share what prominent faculties of CA have to share.

These are all experts. With more years of experience than my number of attempts! They are wise people, and curious people like you and I always listen to the wise people.

Here we go:

Saket Sharma

*M.Com, CS, ATC, Dip.IFRS, Pursuing PHD*

When asked about whether to continue the course after multiple attempts or drop it courageously, Saket believes that it depends on the student and situation. A good idea would be to do whatever is helpful. In his years of experience, Saket has also learnt that learning and developing a skill is more relevant than a professional degree.

Riddhi Shah Chheda

*CA, B.Com*

Riddhi strongly urges students to either continue the course with full dedication or drop it. "CA is not for the faint hearted," Riddhi suggests, "although I did not know this when I pursued it myself. Fortunately, I cleared my CA exams in the first attempt, but that is truly not the case with close to 90% of the students who appear. Failing teaches you a lot, maybe I learnt that the hard way, when students of mine could not clear a few papers, or were stuck not able to score the aggregate required." She goes on to add about failure, "It is always more heartbreaking when your student fails to succeed, even more difficult when they are struggling to pick a side. I always offer my help to any student in need, whether during or after the course."

If a student is struggling with a professional degree, Riddhi suggests that it is tough, massively frustrating and consumes all of your energy trying to really understand the key reasons for failure. Her easiest advice would be to talk to someone who understands what you are going through, try to find a way to resolve it and work hard for the degree. However, if at any point, your brain gives up a little, it should be your heart that must motivate you to push yourself. If that also does not happen, maybe the course is not right for you.

"Maybe it's difficult to hear this coming from me," Riddhi says, who has devoted her life to teaching, "but I wish that students should not forget that this is just a degree. There are many more degrees, jobs, options to choose from always. One exam is not the end of your career, definitely, not the end of the world."

Sunil Shenoy

*CA, B.Com*

Offering a rational approach to quitting or continuing, Sunil says it is a factor of everyone's circumstances. However, he does believe that ambitions do have an expiry date if not accomplished timely. For anyone struggling with anything, Sunil's wisdom says it is wise to let go of things out of reach. Man of few and precise words, I'd say.

Rahul Garg

*FCA, LCS, FCMA, CFA, DISA, B. Com, Adv Dip Mgt.*

Suggesting to drop the course courageously if you are struggling, Rahul says, "In a professional course like CA where the passing percentage is too low, even the bright students face tough times. And after day and night's hard work, some become Chartered Accountants and then, for them the sky is the limit but there are many who in spite of continuous dedicated efforts are unable to win this uphill battle. Thus, a little bit of frustration and depression is normal during the studies especially when encountering failures again and again." Rahul continues, "However, one needs to understand that CA is not the end of the world. Keep a bigger and clear picture in mind that whatever you do, the end goal is to be happy in doing that along with earning decent money. Sometimes, students have fear in mind like what will the parents, relatives and others think when they come to know that you have decided to quit, but at the end of day its your life and you must have that belief in your abilities in general that *'Its ok, may be am not made for this but yes I can succeed in other area where I may relate'*. (Remember Farhan Qureshi, the photographer from 3 Idiots!)?"

Rahul continues his candid contention:

"It's very much possible that you are not made for CA, you may have any other interest area of which you were not aware until this age and its perfectly normal. There is no big deal if you did not identify your interest in the age in which other famous public figures like Sachin Tendulkar did. What bad will it do if you start a little late? There is no race, we all are on our journey in this beautiful world and everyone's journey is different from the other. Moreover, there are a plethora of other options to be chosen from in this modern evolving world. The economies are opening up like never before creating a heaven of opportunities and with the quantum of hard work as done during CA Course, one can break all barriers and challenge all limits. Thus, my honest piece of advice to all the aspirants is that, if you enter a particular field, keep certain success parameters and timelines in your mind on the basis of which you may evaluate your progress and take timely decisions as to whether to continue or make a smart switch. Just remember *'Life is Beautiful'* and don't lose its charm by being stubborn and sticking to one option even on continuous failures, when you can win the world by excelling in other areas of your interest."

Hitesh Satish Sharma

*CA, B.Com (Graduated from HR College)*

Contrary to popular opinion, Hitesh offers to continue the course with full dedication. He advises: "Plan your studies in a better way. Prioritise your degree and make your plan around your study schedule. Surround yourself with positive energies and before going to sleep, talk to yourself for 2-3 minutes and ask whether i was better than yesterday, for my future to be good tomorrow."

For those struggling with where they are, he offers a piece of advice worth its weight in gold: "You will always learn with failures. Take the result on the chin and move on. There was always a reason you couldn't clear, accept and rectify the mistakes.

Increase your self-confidence, stay away from social media which hardly gives positivity when required."

...

My intent with sharing these pieces of advice with you was to make sure you heard not only from me, but also from everyone who has walked the path and also seen thousands of other students walking the path or even discontinuing.

I am sure their words will give you a confidence that will make you move mountains in your own monomaniacal way.

With this, let me take you to the last part of my career so far, on how I created a success for myself, after the unending failures of more than 5 years.

# Chapter 29

# 2023 and Onwards - The Other Side of Drishti

January 2023, the CA results were announced. By the next month, I realised discontinuing CA was a decision I was merely postponing. So, I finally decided to figure something else out.

This was also the time content creation as a full-time profession was booming like crazy. The first thing I started was my own Instagram handle of @ bizzwithdrishti that spoke about BEST (Business, Economics, Strategy and Technology).

The next month of my research phase I came across a course on Scrum. Since it operated at an intersection of management and technology, I enrolled for the course. Well, staying true to myself, I figured out what the course was about, despite having no initial knowledge.

During a mini-break of the two-day course, the instructor wanted to know more about me. More so, because most of the applicants were from IT background and I was the anomaly with a Commerce background.

*Guess what? He was looking for someone to join for the Founder's Office role in his startup, and found me to be a great fit.*

*__In a series of interviews and synchrodestinies, I joined my first ever full-time job on 8<sup>th</sup> of March 2023.__*

When people say curiosity leads you to places, they mean it literally! Had I not enrolled in something I was curious about, maybe I would still be banging my head against the wall.

Since I turned 23 on 17th of March, I can very well say that I started working at the age of 22!!

The following months, I was also invited to be a judge on two different events of CA students.

A funny thing that happened was, I was addressed as "CA Drishti Bajaj" in one of the emails. I thought this was a sign from the universe to start working for CA again. But then I thought the universe had already given me countless signs in those 5 years, which I ignored blindly.

Not this time. Not this time, Drishti.

In July of the same year, I got my first smartphone Google Pixel 7 from my savings. In October of that year, I sponsored my very first to-and-fro domestic flight to Delhi. I also did some shopping from my own money, even if it was Sarojini Nagar for now :) The most surreal feeling, though, was getting gifts for Mom and Bua on my way home. Nothing could match that feeling.

A year later, in March 2024, I visited my sister and Jiju in Boston, by sponsoring my own international flight! I visited the education Mecca, Boston, went on to Harvard University, Northeastern University witnessing beautiful mornings and sunrises, and sipped coffee with my sister.

I also worked on planning this book, with a sister from another mother that I found on LinkedIn. She is also the editor of this book.

As I write this book, I have also been writing and reaching out to people who would be willing to post about my book on their socials and spread a word about it in their gatherings. This book is not just my story, but a 7-year transformation and what it changed in me.

This book is a hope that firsts can go wrong, seconds, thirds and a few other bets on you as well, but life my dear friend, is not a zero-sum game.

Something, some fate or a career trajectory that you may be unaware of would take an asymmetrical bet on you which makes the risk high but rewards even higher.

At the same time, I have also begun to take early career calls from students looking to get out of a loop and invest their 20s for a better experiential learning. I am utilizing this timeframe to prepare my B-school applications, because why not! What is life if it is devoid of education?

And I am keen to work with individuals and build a solution for career shift/switch in India.

Where conventional paths can be chosen but not necessarily be followed. Writing my GMAT and preparing for my Arangetram, which is the graduation in bharatnatyam on the side as well.

Who knows, if you reach out to me in 2027, I might be a full-time dancer as a professional!

Which is why, I truly hope this book reaches the right hands and helps people build that courage to take one step at a time.

To know which schools value a holistic profile and are ready to take an asymmetrical bet on me or if you need any counselling, feel free to ping me on LinkedIn. I have also been reaching out to publishers and still facing rejections because my audience is still not the numbers they are looking at, but I guess, it will all be immaterial once the book is out and the universe does its job! Like it always does. Every single time. Without fail.

# Chapter 30

# 10 Unusual Life Lessons from the Journey of 7 Years

*1. Taking absolutely zero opinions from people about a goal you cannot share with them.*

I did not take advice from my own mother during CA, not because she was wrong. But because I could not explain to her what I was going through. Perhaps I didn't try as well. She was always available for me but as a mother not a mentor. Perhaps she would have been able to provide her inputs had I taken the time to share what was on my mind.

*2. Holding people accountable on face value.*

During 8 am lectures, professors who entered the class at 7:55 am and waited till 8:00 am had my utmost respect. But professors who entered at 8:15 am after a tea booster for the session did not make me feel good about them.

Respect isn't an age or education specific emotion. It is a life value that flows regardless of either.

### 3. *Penning down good/bad feelings about your day at the fag end of your day is like treating your brain with freedom of thoughts.*

When you write a mock test and are not able to perform well, you should write about your feelings with the exact plan of how you would approach this problem the next day. Maybe you went blank, did not recollect the formulae, were anxious, were facing a time crunch whatever it is.

A thought written with a pen on a diary is a reflection of your mind, it clears the voices to a great extent.

Vent out to be cleared out. It serves as a fertile soil for new, important seeds to fertilize in.

### 4. *Frameworks take you to places.*

Visiting my substack handle, "Beyond9to5" will make you the BEST in Business, Economics, Strategy and Technology.

This is not an acronym or a full form, this is the human mindset of taking things seriously when put in frameworks.

The newsletter, "Beyond 9 to 5" covers my weekly strategic picks, has a content corner where I post content from the fields of BEST and also has a corporate wellness section. This section gives you recipes to cook using basic ingredients under 20 minutes. (A little more than Zepto but in a healthy way)

Why do you think management consultants are obsessed with frameworks?

They want to first complicate businesses run by somebody 2x their age and experience and simplify it for them!

### 5. Advices are free to give and opinions are easier to make.

Always ensure you have data backed up for the advice you give and a valid reason to believe in the opinion you say out loud.

Giving an opinion on someone says more about you than the other person.

So is not giving an opinion and asking questions, out of empathy and curiosity to know more.

You choose. In every single interaction.

### 6. Post Covid-19 we are living in such a borderless nation that we have access to the global world on a URL.

Covid taught us the importance of work from home. Prior to Covid-19 we would be at physical locations, travel all our way and do the obvious things.

Be grateful you are living in this era of freedom and flexibility, and adapt to the ever- changing dynamics. Don't be fixated on things. Evolve.

**7.   *In your 20s when you think of wealth, please don't think about money alone.***

Plan your finances well, save and invest. But do not forget to get a saree or a suit for your mother.

The joy hits differently. Those moments are priceless.

Think about your time wealth as well.

Plan to free up your time. Do things that add value to your skillset.

If resources are not a constraint, upskill regularly. Do not wait for "on the job" training.

If at all, you feel, even if I put in 2 years into this task - some other person would do it better. Blindly outsource it.

You are not lazy here, trust me.

You are sharpening your axe for what you can cut better.

There is absolutely no point in practising a craftsmanship that is not designed for you.


**8.   *Geet ko Aditya train chootne par hi mila tha, isliye kuch kaam chootne do na!***

When you feel stuck at a place and are frustrated with the feeling of not being able to move forward, let it go.

Move on from the phase, do not delete that feeling.

This undeleted feeling will motivate you to perform better at other things in life.

Through the book you must have realised by now, that I was stuck to CA as a course. However, ever since I decided to move on from the course, I could potentially add much more to my character. I could build depth in my thinking, however, I am still a very anxious individual, however I do not make decisions in haste or FOMO anymore.

During the CA journey, the day I got my results, I would order for fasttrack lectures/ updated material and what not.

However, I now understand the importance of "Pause and Reflect".

Reflecting is a superpower. Reacting is simply a nonsense approach in life.

### 9. *In life, do yourself a favour - control your overthinking.*

Understand that the result of anything in life is a combination of possibility and probability.

Do not interpret both as one.

The possibility of 'A' happening is 100% however, the probability of 'A' happening in a certain way is not 100%

It cannot be.

Because if it's so certain to happen, you would not be overthinking about it. You would be sure of it.

And if you are so sure about certain things, if they are not happening your way, learn to deal with the consequences.

Find solutions.

Remember—There's always a solution.

## 10. Ending this book is like bidding goodbye to a piece of my heart.

But in the end, all I want to say is, you are the sum product of the choices you make and the kindness you share with the world out there.

Stay humble, stay grounded and stay hydrated.

…

Return to these 10 cheat codes each time you feel stuck in life, and you will find a solution. Try it out for yourself.

A bonus lesson, because I believe in giving a little 'extra'.

Practice being aware. Practice being in the moment. Practice Optimism. Life will seem a little more sorted.

These golden words are coming from failing, failing umpteen times and gathering courage to show up in silence.

# About the Author

Drishti is a 25-year-old, born and brought up in Mumbai. She wears multiple hats of a growth marketeer during the day, consults content ninjas by the night.

She is a drama fanatic, through and through. Stage and a mic are her go-to buddies.

She proudly says that if her DNA were decoded, it would spell out her ABCs – Art, Business, and Content.

Drishti focuses on what is to be aware in the moment, forgetting the past and tries to worry less of the future.

She claims this is her newly acquired trait.

Writing and expressing emotions is her way to connect people. Drishti has been terrible at her professional exams. This was because she wanted to be at 10 places and was never taught the skill of being present in the moment. All she was doing was planning her next move.

So, she set out to write a book for her younger self, sharing everything about how to plan things better for professional success in the early stage of adulting.

Pure Insight. Action Oriented.

Not for the light-hearted.

Discover how to navigate the space of professional exams, one day at a time. Learn how to shut the noise and chase success to come to you!

www.ingramcontent.com/pod-product-compliance
Lightning Source LLC
Chambersburg PA
CBHW031300130726
47988CB00007B/2662